DAVID J. BREEZE

ROMAN FORTS
IN BRITAIN

SHIRE ARCHAEOLOGY

Cover photograph
The reconstructed gate at the Lunt fort, Baginton, near Coventry, with the
granary visible inside the fort. This reconstruction was based on the fort gates
depicted on Trajan's Column.
(Photograph by Cadbury Lamb, taken by permission of
Coventry City Council.)

Published in 1994 by
SHIRE PUBLICATIONS LTD
Cromwell House, Church Street, Princes Risborough,
Buckinghamshire HP27 9AJ, UK.

Series Editor: James Dyer

ISBN 0 85263 654 7

First edition 1983; reprinted 1987; reprinted with amendments 1994.

Printed in Great Britain by
CIT Printing Services, Press Buildings,
Merlins Bridge, Haverfordwest, Dyfed SA61 1XF.

Contents

LIST OF ILLUSTRATIONS   4

PREFACE   5

1. THE ROMAN FORT: A DESCRIPTION   7

2. THE CAMP   9

3. THE FORT   13

4. FORTS, FORTRESSES, FORTLETS AND TOWERS   23

5. BUILDING THE FORT   47

6. LIFE IN THE FORT   53

7. SELECT GAZETTEER   63

8. FURTHER READING   68

INDEX   71

Acknowledgements

I am most grateful to Drs Brian Dobson, W. S. Hanson and Valerie A. Maxfield for reading the text of this book in draft and for their most useful comments, to Mr Dennis Gallagher for drawing figs. 1, 4, 5, 7, 11, 12, 15, 20, 23, 27, 35 and 43, to Mr Michael J. Moore for figs. 24, 26, 29, 34 and 36, and to Mr C. M. Daniels for allowing me to use his work on Housesteads as a basis for fig. 1. I am also grateful to the following for permission to reproduce illustrations: National Monuments Record of Scotland (2 and 45), National Museum of Antiquities of Scotland (3 and 40), Committee for Aerial Photography, Cambridge University (6, 10, 13, 30, 32, 41, 44 and 46), Ministry of Defence (6 and 32), Museum of Antiquities, Newcastle upon Tyne (9 and 19), Dr Valerie A. Maxfield (17 and 18), Scottish Development Department (Ancient Monuments Division) (27 and 38), Society for the Promotion of Roman Studies (31), Mr A. Lamb (37 and 39) and Tyne and Wear Museums Service (47).

List of illustrations

Cover. The reconstructed timber gate at the Lunt, Baginton
1. Plan of Housesteads fort *page 6*
2. The camps at Pennymuir from the air *page 8*
3. Tent peg and mallet *page 10*
4. Plans of marching camps *page 11*
5. Plan of the supply base at South Shields *page 12*
6. The fort at Hod Hill from the air *page 12*
7. Plan of the fort at the Lunt, Baginton *page 16*
8. Map of southern Scotland in the late first century AD *page 19*
9. A model of the fort at Benwell *page 20*
10. The fort at Portchester from the air *page 21*
11. Plan of Pevensey fort *page 22*
12. Plan of Bearsden fort *page 24*
13. The fort at Housesteads from the air *page 25*
14. The reconstructed walls of the fort at Cardiff *page 26*
15. Plan of the headquarters building at Housesteads *page 26*
16. The strongroom at Chesters *page 28*
17. A screen in a rear room in the headquarters building at Chesterholm-*Vindolanda* *page 28*
18. The tribunal in the headquarters building at Chesterholm-*Vindolanda* *page 29*
19. Sculpture of Mars from the headquarters building at Housesteads *page 29*
20. Plan of the commanding officer's house at Housesteads *page 30*
21. The reconstructed timber granary at the Lunt, Baginton *page 31*
22. The north granary at Housesteads *page 32*
23. Plans of barrack-blocks *page 33*
24. A pair of barrack-blocks at Chesters *page 35*
25. The latrine block at Housesteads *page 36*
26. Reconstruction of the interior of the latrine at Bearsden *page 37*
27. Plans of the bath-houses at Chesters and Bearsden *page 38*
28. The bath-house at Bearsden *page 39*
29. A reconstruction drawing of the fort at Rough Castle *page 39*
30. Aerial view of the fort and parade ground at Hardknott *page 40*
31. Plan of the fortress at Inchtuthil *page 41*
32. Aerial view of the amphitheatre at Caerleon *page 43*
33. Plan of the fortlet at Barburgh Mill *page 44*
34. A reconstruction drawing of the fortlet at Barburgh Mill *page 44*
35. Plans of the towers at Parkneuk and Scarborough *page 45*
36. A reconstruction drawing of the tower at Parkneuk *page 45*
37. Trajan's Column: legionaries building *page 48*
38. A building inscription from Bearsden *page 49*
39. Trajan's Column: legionaries building *page 50*
40. Carpenter's tools from Newstead *page 51*
41. Aerial view of the Roman camp and iron age hillfort at Burnswark *page 52*
42. The temple of Mithras at Carrawburgh *page 52*
43. Plan of the civil settlement at Old Carlisle *page 55*
44. Aerial view of the fort and civil settlement at Chesterholm-*Vindolanda* *page 56*
45. The fort at Ardoch from the air *page 60*
46. The fort at Caernarfon from the air *page 62*
47. The rebuilt gate at South Shields *page 67*

Preface

The Roman fort is an evocative reminder of one of the world's greatest empires. The earthworks of Ardoch in Perthshire, the fort at Housesteads on Hadrian's Wall with its impressive array of internal buildings or the towering walls of Portchester on the Saxon Shore, even in decline, impress even the most casual visitor. These forts, and the many others visible in Britain, are a tangible expression of the power and discipline of the greatest army the world has seen.

The purpose of this book is to describe the Roman fort in Britain, outlining its development and discussing its role. The frontiers to which some forts were attached, for example Hadrian's Wall, are not discussed. A further aspect of military life can be found in *Roman Roads,* by Richard W. Bagshawe, also in the Shire Archaeology series.

This book starts with a description of a Roman fort, Housesteads on Hadrian's Wall, in order to provide a background for the ensuing discussion. A chapter on the camp is concerned with temporary installations, and this is followed by a discussion of the development of the fort in Britain. In the third chapter forts, fortresses, fortlets and watch-towers, together with their internal buildings, are described. Sections on building the fort and life in the fort follow. A gazetteer indicates those sites where military remains are still visible. Wherever possible the illustrations in the text are of forts with visible remains. Finally there are suggestions for further reading.

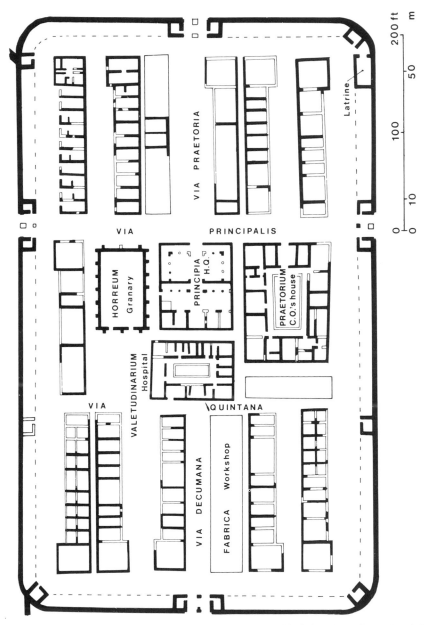

1. Plan of the fort at Housesteads on Hadrian's Wall. This is based on C. M. Daniel's interpretation of R. C. Bosanquet's 1898 plan. Of the barrack-blocks only the two in the top left-hand (north-east) corner have been completely excavated. The incomplete plans of the others suggest that each barrack-block was divided into ten rooms, each in turn subdivided into two, and an officer's block.

1
The Roman fort: a description

It is a common misconception that all Roman forts were built to a standard design. No two Roman forts are the same, and even those on Hadrian's Wall, which have many features in common, are different in many other ways. The reasons for this are that forts were built by different units, at different times, for different garrisons. The forts on Hadrian's Wall are unusual in that most appear to have been built for single auxiliary units. Many forts at other times were built for either a composite garrison or a detachment from another fort. This introduces a wide variety of possible building plans. Further, fort design and layout changed over the centuries: there is a considerable difference between a fort constructed in the aftermath of the invasion of Britain in AD 43 and a Saxon Shore fort built 250 years later. For these reasons it would be misleading to try to categorise forts too closely, to write of 'fort types'.

There will therefore be no attempt to provide fort plans for different types of units. Rather those forts with particularly informative or interesting plans will be illustrated. In spite of all the differences most forts shared basic common features, in both the defences and the internal buildings, and this applies particularly to the forts of the first and second centuries. To provide the necessary background for the ensuing discussion, a restored plan of Housesteads is used as the frame for a description of the basic features of the Roman fort built in the first and second centuries.

Roman forts usually faced the enemy, the line of march, or east: Housesteads faced east. The defences usually consisted of a rampart of turf or stone with at least two ditches: at Housesteads the stone wall was backed by an earthen rampart. The walls were pierced by four gates. The main gate was the *porta praetoria,* the rear gate the *porta decumana,* and the side gates the *porta principalis sinistra* and *porta principalis dextra.* These led to roads: the *via praetoria* leading into the fort from the main gate; the *via principalis* crossing the fort between the two side gates; and the *via decumana* which led in from the rear gate and met, at right angles, a subsidiary road, the *via quintana,* which ran behind the central range of buildings in the fort. Inside the rampart a road, the *via sagularis,* or *intervallum* road, ran round the whole circuit of the fort.

The area forward of the *via principalis* was termed the *praetentura,* and that behind the *via quintana* was called the *retentura.* The principal buildings normally faced on to the *via principalis.* These included the headquarters *(principia)* placed in the centre of the fort, with, usually to the right, the commanding officer's house *(praetorium)* and to the left the granaries *(horrea).* Also in the central range there might be a hospital *(valetudinarium)* and workshop *(fabrica).* The headquarters housed the offices of the regimental clerks, the temple containing the standards of the unit, the strongroom, a hall for regimental assemblies and a courtyard.

The rest of the fort was primarily devoted to barrack-blocks. Each fort usually contained at least six, and these were divided into small rooms, each normally occupied by eight soldiers, and a larger suite for the centurion or decurion. In addition there were storehouses and stables for the cavalry mounts and mules.

The bath-house was generally placed outside the fort, sometimes in an annexe, though the latrine was probably usually situated in a corner of the fort.

2. The marching camps at Pennymuir looking north: the smaller camp lies in the right-hand corner of the larger. Both camps had the same arrangement of entrances: one on each of the shorter sides and two on the other sides. All entrances were protected by a detached section of rampart and ditch, a *titulum.* (Crown Copyright.)

2
The camp

The Roman army, apparently from the earliest days, was trained to throw up temporary defences to protect itself when on campaign. These marching camps were simple structures consisting of a ditch fronting a bank formed from the material dug out of the ditch: extra defence was created by the emplanting of stakes in the top of the rampart — each soldier carried two for this purpose. The anonymous compiler of the military treatise *De Metatione Castrorum,* writing in the first or second century AD, states that the minimum width of the ditch should be 5 Roman feet and the depth 3 feet, while the minimum width of the rampart should be 8 feet and the height 6 feet. The entrances were wide gaps defended by a detached section of rampart and ditch (a *titulum*) or a hook curving round one side of the gap (a *clavicula*). In certain cases it seems that temporary timber gates were constructed.

Within the defences, the camp was crossed by wide roads. These divided the camp into areas assigned to the general staff and the troops on campaign. An advance party marked out the position of the defences, roads and other internal arrangements with flags and each unit, as it arrived, marched to its pre-ordained location. The first task was to construct the defences, the diggers being protected by a screen of soldiers. On completion of the defences all soldiers retired within the camp to pitch the tents. The senior officers were accommodated in the centre of the camp and around them lay the smaller tents of the soldiers, in rows, century facing century across the side roads of the camp (see figs. 23 and 24). The arrangement for the century, at this time consisting of eighty men, is described in *De Metatione Castrorum.* Each century was issued with eight tents, eight soldiers being assigned to one tent: only sixty-four men were thus provided for as sixteen were on guard duty at any one time and used the bedding of their colleagues when they came off duty. Each tent measured 10 feet square and the soldiers placed their arms on the ground in front of the tent. At the end of the row was a large tent for the centurion.

The camp provided protection against the surprise attack. At the same time the wide internal streets and the broad space between the rampart and the tents facilitated movement within the camp and allowed the army to assemble quickly and easily, while the broad entrances provided for ready access to the enemy. The Roman army was an offensive army, used to fighting — and winning — in the open: this is clearly reflected in the arrangement of the temporary camp.

3. A tent peg and mallet from Newstead (the rope and haft are modern).

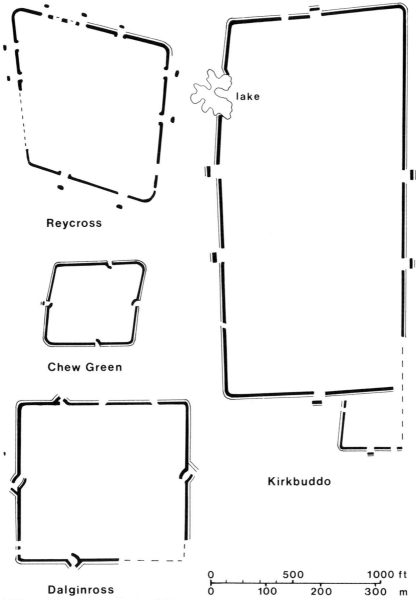

Reycross

Chew Green

Dalginross

lake

Kirkbuddo

0		500		1000 ft
0	100	200	300	m

4. Plans of four marching camps in north Britain. The entrances at first-century Reycross and third-century Kirkbuddo are protected by *titula*. At Chew Green the entrances have internal *claviculae:* one, in addition, has a *titulum*. The entrances at first-century Dalginross are complicated with both internal and external *claviculae*. The nearly square shape of Reycross and Dalginross reflects their date of construction, while Kirkbuddo is representative of the oblong third-century camps.

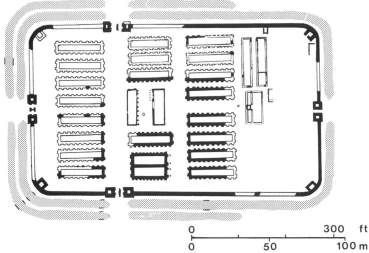

0	300 ft
0	50 100 m

5. The fort at South Shields at the mouth of the Tyne was turned into a supply base in the early third century when the army was campaigning in Scotland. The barrack-blocks were demolished and replaced by granaries: a total of twenty-two have been located or can be inferred within the fort.

6. Hod Hill, Dorset. The Roman fort was placed in the corner of an iron age hillfort. Although such a location is rare, there are a number of other examples of the reuse of a hillfort in this way in south-west England. Within the complex defences traces of the streets and buildings are visible, revealing that the fort faced east (left). (Crown Copyright.)

3
The fort

Introduction

The camp was intended to provide protection during a brief stay, often merely overnight, but for tasks of longer duration more permanent accommodation was required. In the second century BC, for example, during several sieges of Numantia in Spain the army constructed semi-permanent quarters while in the first century BC Caesar recorded that thatched huts provided shelter in the winter camps of his legions in Gaul. However, forts were rarely mentioned in the literary sources of the late Republic. This may be because the writers were not concerned with such matters, or perhaps few forts existed. A permanent army was only now in process of coming into being and cannot be said to have formally existed until the time of Augustus (27 BC to AD 14). In the main, therefore, the army moved between summer and winter camps. Forts might be built to guard a river crossing or possible invasion routes or other strategic points, but these were temporary constructions, abandoned at the end of the campaign if not at the end of each season. A network of forts was superfluous for the enemy was controlled by the threat of the army's presence, the confiscation of weapons and the taking of hostages, rather than by the physical presence of a relatively small group of men. In any case the division of the army into small task forces emplanted in hostile or recently conquered territory would be dangerous to the soldiers themselves, while severely restricting the manoeuvrability of the army. One charge against Quintilius Varus, who lost three legions in the Teutoberg Forest in Germany in AD 9, was that he had weakened his army by sending men away to protect friendly tribes.

In general, therefore, units were clustered together in large army groups. One such group lay at Antioch, some distance behind the eastern frontier, but carefully positioned to control the main caravan routes from Persia and the East. Other groups lay on the Rhine, poised for the proposed invasion of Germany, a project mortally damaged in AD 9, though it was not realised at the time. Here the nodal point of each concentration was the legionary fortress where one or two legions were stationed, and around this lay the smaller forts of the auxiliary units. As the forts were temporary the buildings were constructed of timber and the defences of earth or turf: they were probably little different from the winter camps.

The first major expansion of the empire following the Varan disaster of AD 9 was the invasion and conquest of Britain. It was in order to gain military prestige and thus bolster his shaky position on the throne that the Emperor Claudius (41-54) ordered the invasion of the island.

Roman armies crossed the English Channel in AD 43 and in the same year the main tribe of southern England, the Catuvellauni, and several other tribes submitted. It was not for another forty years, however, that the province reached its widest extent, when the governor Agricola defeated the Caledonians at Mons Graupius. During these years the army in Britain was constantly on the move, marching, fighting and building. The successive moves forward of the frontier and the resulting construction of new forts facilitate the detailed study of Roman military planning and building. Further, owing to the long history of archaeological excavation in Britain, the province is furnished with a wealth of information provided by the toil of countless diggers.

The Roman army

The Roman army in Britain comprised four (later three) legions — some twenty thousand men — and a similar number of soldiers in the auxiliary units. The legions provided the backbone of the army. Each consisted of a little over five thousand infantrymen, with a small detachment of one hundred and twenty cavalry. These soldiers were armed with the short stabbing sword or *gladius* and two javelins or *pila* and were well protected by body armour and a carefully designed helmet. The legionaries were highly trained and disciplined, used to fighting the set-piece battle. Each legion was divided into ten cohorts, each of four hundred and eighty men, though the first cohort was later modified to be double in size (actually eight hundred, not nine hundred and sixty strong), and the cohorts were in turn divided into centuries of eighty men apiece. The legion was commanded by a legate, a senator in his early thirties, supported by one senior tribune (a young man in his late teens or early twenties), a prefect and five junior tribunes, all from the lesser or equestrian nobility. All appointments were usually held for about three years. One officer stood out from the rest, the prefect of the camp. He was a long-serving soldier in his fifties or sixties, who had risen from the ranks of the centurionate: this man more than any other was responsible for the smooth operation of the legion, for his senior colleagues all held what today would be regarded as short-term commissions. The legionary cohort did not have a commanding officer, so the next grade below the junior tribune was the centurion, the officer in charge of the century. Although some centurions entered the army by direct commission, most had risen from the ranks. These sixty officers formed the core of the legion. They were supported by their own junior officers, soldiers who themselves aspired to be centurions. The legion did not just contain soldiers: it included within its ranks its own medical corps, artillery, and building and maintenance staff.

Support for the legions came from the auxiliary (literally 'support') units. These had originally been raised from amongst the friends and allies of Rome, but by AD 43 they were recruited mainly from the frontier tribes of the empire. They were organised into units about five hundred strong (quingenary) and could be either infantry or cavalry, or both. The infantry cohort probably nominally contained four hundred and eighty men, the cavalry regiment *(ala)* five hundred and twelve and the mixed cohort six hundred and eight, though surviving army documents reveal that units could be under strength by as much as twenty-five per cent. In the last thirty years of the first century new types of auxiliary units were created. These were approximately twice the size of the existing units, being about eight hundred, seven hundred and sixty-eight and one thousand and fifty-six strong, respectively. All milliary (thousand) units were rare: there was never more than one *ala milliaria* per province. The most common unit in the British army was the *cohors quingenaria equitata,* the small mixed infantry and cavalry unit, between one third and one half of the regiments in Britain being of this size.

Each auxiliary regiment was commanded by a prefect or tribune, equal in rank to the junior tribunes in the legion. The infantry were divided into centuries, probably eighty strong, each commanded by a centurion, and the cavalry into troops, each of thirty-two men and commanded by a decurion. As in the legions these officers had generally been promoted from the ranks.

Forts in Britain
Our knowledge of the disposition of Roman forces in Britain in the early years of the conquest is slight, and our understanding of the forts themselves even more hazy. The forts should have been little more than winter quarters, for in the summer the army

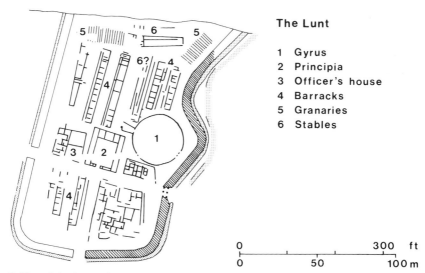

The Lunt

1 Gyrus
2 Principia
3 Officer's house
4 Barracks
5 Granaries
6 Stables

```
0                          300   ft
0              50          100 m
```

7. Plan of the fort at the Lunt, Baginton, probably built in the 60s. The fort was reduced in size following the construction of the circular enclosure: this accounts for the curve of the east rampart. The enclosure may have been used for breaking in horses (a *gyrus*).

would have been out on campaign. In a rare instance, at Metchley near Birmingham, the drainage gullies between the tents of such troops have been recognised during excavation. The troops, unusually, slept in tents while mopping up the last resistance in the winter following the Boudican revolt. Normally, no doubt, huts were constructed in the manner recorded by Caesar in Gaul or for Corbulo in Cappadocia. While these enclosures cannot be dignified with the name 'fort', so the troops stationed there were not 'garrisons'. The winter quarters would serve as the home of a group of soldiers over the winter months, but that group might consist of one or more units, or part of a unit, and might retire to a different site, and in a different combination of units, the following autumn. In such circumstances frequent modifications are to be expected and indeed have been recorded at some early 'fort' sites.

It is difficult to determine the precise point at which a winter camp became a permanent fort. Structurally the two might be very similar, the defences comprising ditches and an earthen rampart with timber gates and towers, while the internal buildings would be of timber, with little noticeable difference between 'temporary' and 'permanent' buildings. The establishment of the same regular unit stationed within the winter quarters might be considered the turning point, but that date is not recognisable either archaeologically or through the pitifully small documentary record. Thus, for the sake of convenience, the enclosures described below are termed 'forts' rather than 'winter quarters'.

The literary sources for the conquest period record — or hint at — the disposition of the four legions of the province. One legion was established at the provincial capital, Colchester, formerly the capital of the main enemy of Rome, the Catuvellauni/Trinovantes. The other three seem to have been strategically placed for attack and defence; one in the south-west, the second in the west midlands, and the third in the east midlands. The position of the auxiliary units is not clear. Military equipment has been found at many sites in southern England, but insufficient is known to be able to ascertain whether in the main the auxiliary units were concentrated round the legions, or spread out across the countryside, or placed close to the provincial boundary. There is no doubt, however, of the function of these units: their aim was to protect the province from attack and police the new provincials. The provincials need not be controlled by the establishment of forts in their territory: the taking of hostages, the confiscation of weapons and the threat of the army's presence would normally be sufficient to maintain order. No barrier was constructed along the frontier, for that would have been superfluous: rather the units would have been positioned with an eye to the best lines of communication and supply.

The bases of the early years of the conquest varied considerably in size from Nanstallan at 2.2 acres (0.89 ha) through 4 to 7 acre (1.6 to 2.8 ha) (auxiliary) forts to large enclosures covering 20 to 26 acres (8.1 to 10.5 ha) and legionary fortresses of 40 to 50 acres (16 to 20 ha). On excavation, such sites have generally revealed traces of normal military buildings, such as barrack-blocks and the headquarters building, but some of the larger enclosures have yielded evidence only of stores buildings or workshops.

The pattern of occupation of newly conquered territory is more clearly seen with the subjugation of Wales and north Britain in the 70s and 80s (see fig. 8). Forts were placed about a day's march apart, 14 to 20 miles (22 to 32 km). Most were of a size to hold a single auxiliary unit, though sometimes smaller detachments were used and elsewhere larger forts, presumably holding composite garrisons, were established. The legionary bases were moved forward so that these units could keep in touch with the new areas of activity. While these forts — all built of turf and timber — and the network to which they belong lend an air of permanence to the scene, it must be emphasised that they are still essentially semi-permanent winter quarters: in the summer they would lie abandoned by an army active in the field.

The withdrawal of a legion from Britain in the late 80s was a crucial action for perhaps more than any other single event it ensured that the whole of the island would not succumb to Roman arms. This in turn led to two events: the construction of artificial frontiers to the province, and an immobility which resulted in units remaining in forts for decades and their timber buildings being replaced in stone.

No less than four frontier systems were built in north Britain from the 80s to the 140s and the greatest of these, Hadrian's Wall, underwent numerous modifications through the nearly three hundred years it was occupied. Nevertheless, the construction of these frontiers had no major effect on the disposition of the troops of the provincial army, for the two served different purposes. The frontiers were essentially bureaucratic in concept: their purpose was to allow the army to control the movement of people into and out of the province and thus help prevent petty raiding and the like. Although both Hadrian's Wall and the Antonine Wall clearly had a defensive capability, they would only slow rather than halt major attacks. The army was therefore disposed, as before, to defend the province from such attacks, as well as maintain internal order in the frontier area. The only change in military dispositions — apart from the movement into Scotland and then back — was unrelated to the building of the Walls, and that is the thickening of the outer band of forts by the reduction in the distance between these forts from a day's march apart to half a day's march — 7 miles (11 km) or thereabouts — presumably in order to aid the duties of frontier control. And as the provincials behind the frontier became more peaceful, the units in the hinterland became less an occupation force and more a support for the troops in the front line.

The second change, rebuilding in stone, did not happen at once. Forts were rebuilt piecemeal as their turf or earth ramparts required refacing and their timber buildings replacing. But at the same time — in the early years of the second century — some new forts were built partly or wholly in stone. On Hadrian's Wall, for example, about half the forts were built of stone (see fig. 9), while the rest were of turf and timber. Even the so-called stone forts were not completely of stone: they were surrounded by stone

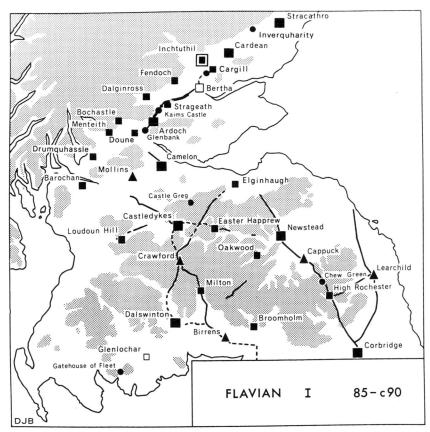

8. Southern Scotland in the late first century. South of the Forth-Clyde isthmus, large forts were established in the main river valleys with smaller forts and fortlets in between. North of the isthmus the topography forced a different solution. Here one line of forts lay along the road leading north. The purpose of the outer line is not clear: the forts may have been built to guard the mouths of the Highland glens, or they may have been planned as the springboard for an advance up the glens, an advance prevented by the withdrawal of a legion from Britain and the subsequent abandonment of the fortress at Inchtuthil.

walls and their principal buildings were of stone, but the barrack-blocks and storehouses were either wholly of timber, or of timber placed on low sill walls. This pattern continued into the second century and beyond. Most of the forts on the Antonine Wall had turf ramparts, but their internal buildings were of both stone and timber (see figs. 12 and 29), while many other forts in Lowland Scotland built at this time contained no stone buildings at all. The legionary base constructed at Carpow on the Tay in the

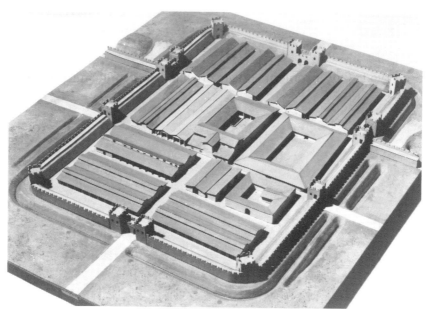

9. A model of the fort at Benwell on Hadrian's Wall. The headquarters building in the centre of the fort is flanked, to right, by the commanding officer's house and, to left, by the granaries and a (?) workshop. The hospital lies behind (i.e. this side of) the commanding officer's house. The rest of the fort is crammed with barrack-blocks, stables and storehouses. The whole is protected by a stone wall and two ditches.

early third century had a turf rampart, stone gates, stone principal buildings and timber barrack-blocks. On Hadrian's Wall many timber buildings appear to have been rebuilt in stone in the third century, but timber was used for new buildings in several forts in the later fourth century. If there is any rule, it appears to be that new forts were generally built in turf and timber (Hadrian's Wall is an exception), though in the second century and later the principal buildings might be of stone, but when timber buildings required replacing they were usually rebuilt in stone.

In the history of Roman forts in Britain the most remarkable changes in military architecture occurred not in the north but on the south and east coasts (see figs. 10 and 11). There had been a small number of forts here for many years, most associated with the British fleet, whose purpose was primarily to maintain military and administrative contact between Britain and the continent. Excavations in the 1970s revealed part of one of these forts at Dover. But in the final quarter of the third century these forts were supplemented by the construction of probably seven new bases. These forts were unlike all earlier military enclosures in Britain. They had high, thick walls, wide, deep ditches and small, heavily defended gates. Some are still exceptionally well preserved. One problem, however, has been to locate buildings within the forts. At Lympne part of the headquarters and a bath-house have been recognised, but extensive excavations at Portchester revealed only slight traces of timber buildings together with pits, wells and ovens. These forts, together with two earlier sites and one later fort, are all listed in a late fourth-century document, the *Notitia Dignitatum,* as being under the command of the Count of the Saxon Shore. However, what precisely the Saxon Shore was and how it operated are matters of

10. Aerial view of the Saxon Shore fort at Portchester. The medieval castle occupies one corner of the defended enclosure. Although the curtain wall was repaired in the medieval period, essentially it seems to be much as when the Romans abandoned the site.

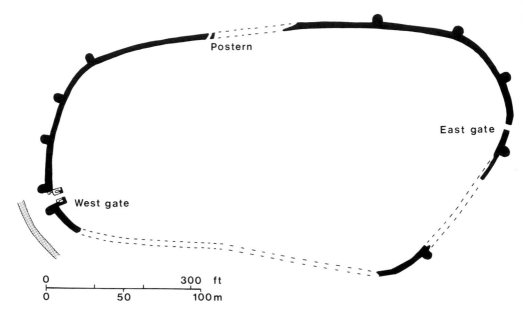

11. The fourth-century Saxon Shore fort at Pevensey departs dramatically from the straight lines of earlier years.

conjecture. Ordinary military units are attested at these sites, but several are in isolated positions, removed from the road network, and must have been supplied by sea. The relationship of the units to the fleet is, however, unclear.

The construction of these forts is an unmistakable step in the decline of the Roman army, from an offensive army based in lightly defended camps or forts, to a defensive organisation reliant upon heavily defended enclosures: it is not surprising that many of these enclosures were reused as castles in the medieval period for that is essentially what they were, and as such they were far removed from the forts of earlier years.

4
Forts, fortresses, fortlets and towers

In this chapter the military installations constructed by the Roman army in Britain are examined in detail.

The fort

Over three hundred auxiliary forts are known in Britain and because at many sites there are several superimposed forts the true number is much higher. Forts for single auxiliary units can range in size from 2 to 10 acres (0.8 to 4.0 ha), though most fall within the range 3.5 to 6 acres (1.4 to 2.4 ha). As many forts held either detachments or composite garrisons, the size of forts can fall to 1 acre (0.4 ha) or rise to 15 acres (6.1 ha): the first-century forts of about 20 to 26 acres (8.1 to 10.5 ha) form a group of their own so far as their size is concerned, though this does not necessarily imply that they were all built for the same purpose.

The regular plan of the fort of the late first to mid second century has already been described (see also fig. 13). In the mid first century and in the later second century the layout tends to be less regular (but see fig. 12). The precise regularity of the 'standard' fort appears to coincide with the years when it seems to be usual for there to be only one unit in each fort. In view of the lack of evidence, nothing can be said about the planning of the coastal forts of the late third and fourth centuries.

Defences of the fort

In the first century the ramparts tended to be of earth or turf. Earthen ramparts were usually revetted at front and rear by turf or timber to prevent slippage. Some were placed on a base or foundation of timber, gravel or occasionally stone: in the mid second century stone foundations became more common and were constructed at many of the new forts in Scotland as well as on the Antonine Wall. Turf or earth ramparts could vary enormously in thickness, though most were between 15 and 25 feet (4.5 and 7.6 m) wide.

Stone walls were generally about 7 feet (2.1 m) wide, though because many were at first merely a new facing to an existing rampart the full thickness of this part of the defences remained as before, while new stone forts were also provided with a rampart backing of earth. Rarely does a wall survive to full height, but a

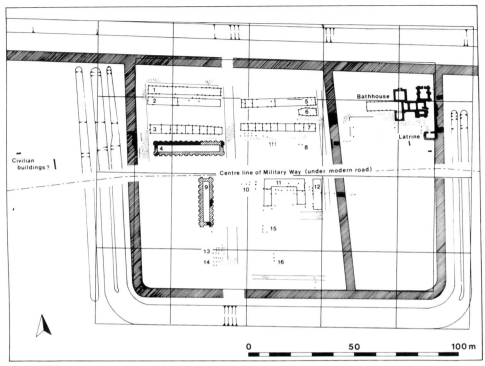

12. Bearsden on the Antonine Wall was built in the mid second century for a detachment. The fort contained barrack-blocks (3 and 7), granaries (4 and 9), a storehouse (12), and probably a workshop (11) and stables (1, 2, 5 and 6); the bath-house lay in an annexe. The layout is irregular but nevertheless planned. The outline of the ditches rests on a grid formed of 5 by 4 *actus* (1 *actus* = 120 Roman feet), while the ramparts follow a grid of 4 by 3 *actus*. The *via principalis* (on the line of the Military Way) falls on the centre line of the grid. Several buildings measure 1 *actus* long, while some are paired and measure ½ *actus* across their outer walls. (The south-west corner of the fort and the south half of the annexe have not been excavated.)

part of the fortress wall at York still stands 15 feet (4.5 m) high and 5 feet (1.5 m) wide to the parapet: the whole wall may have been 20 feet (6.1 m) high. A similar height has been calculated for the wider lengths of Hadrian's Wall. Turf and earth walls may have been rather lower.

The gates in turf or earth ramparts were of timber, generally with two portals or passages, and frequently with guard chambers. The structure normally rose above the rampart to form a tower (see cover). Similar towers were placed at the corners of forts, and sometimes on the sides (see fig. 1). Stone forts were provided with stone towers. The base of the tower in some cases was used for storage or to house ovens.

In the mid second century, although many forts had turf

ramparts, gates and towers were sometimes of stone. The gates were often simple structures without guard chambers, while the size of the posts used in the timber gates suggests that some might not have continued upwards to form a tower.

Beyond the rampart lay the ditches. These were generally two in number, though there might be as many as six, as at Birrens in Dumfriesshire. In shape, they were more often than not V-shaped, sometimes with a slot in the bottom. A refinement was

13. The fort at Housesteads from the air looking west (see fig. 1). The headquarters building in the centre is flanked to left by the commanding officer's house, to right by the granaries, while the hospital lies behind. In the near right-hand corner lie two rows of chalets built in the fourth century. Far left are visible some of the houses in the civil settlement.

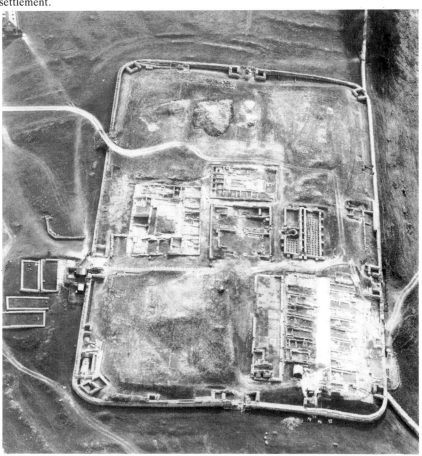

14. The new style forts are not confined to the Saxon Shore but are also found on the west coast of Britain. One of these, Cardiff Castle, was rebuilt in the nineteenth century.

15. Plan of the Housesteads headquarters building.

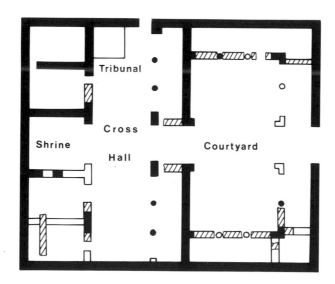

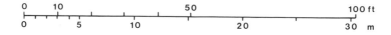

to cut the outer face vertically, to prevent escape: this was termed a Punic ditch. Sometimes extra obstacles were provided in the form of thorn hedges. Most unusually, at Rough Castle on the Antonine Wall several rows of defensive pits or *lilia* were dug to protect the northern approach to the fort: why such pits should have been specially provided here is not known.

The defences of the coastal forts of the late third and fourth centuries are very different from those of the first and second-century forts. Walls 13 feet (4.0 m) wide and 25 feet (7.6 m) high are not uncommon (see fig. 14). Bastions for enfilading fire were normally provided, though sometimes they were a later addition. Entrances were small and well defended.

Headquarters building and commanding officer's house

In the centre of the fort, at the crossing of the *via praetoria* and the *via principalis*, lay the headquarters building *(principia)*. The 'standard' plan called for an open courtyard at the front, surrounded by a verandah, a cross-hall *(basilica)*, and five rooms at the rear (see fig. 15). Mid first-century timber headquarters tend to be simpler, sometimes omitting the cross-hall and possessing only three rooms at the rear and not five (see fig. 7).

The central room at the rear was the focal point of the headquarters. Called the *aedes*, it served as a shrine. Here were a statue of the emperor, the standards of the unit and often an altar. A guard was permanently posted here. As a result the room acquired a further use: the strongroom was placed here (see fig. 16). This frequently took the form of a small underground chamber, with access from the *aedes* or an adjoining room.

The rooms on either side of the *aedes* were used by the administrative staff of the unit. It seems probable that the pay clerks occupied the two rooms to the right and the records clerks those to the left. Sometimes access to the two outer rooms was gained only through the adjacent rooms, and on occasions these were fronted by stone screens surmounted by grills, rather like old-fashioned banks (see fig. 17). Wear on top of the screens suggests the passing of hands — and money — to and fro. The restricted access to the outer rooms may suggest that senior officers worked there: the left-hand room, beside the tribunal, may have been the office of the *cornicularius*, the head of the administrative staff.

In the fourth century hypocausts were inserted into some of the rooms of certain forts. Whether this was to help the clerks keep warm or to allow the rooms to be used for sleeping accommoda-

16. The strongroom at Chesters was placed in one of the rear side rooms of the headquarters building: it was entered from the *aedes*.
17. At Chesterholm-*Vindolanda* one of the rear rooms retains part of its stone screen: this stone would have been balanced by another to the right, resting in the visible groove.

18. *(above).* The lower half of the tribunal in the *basilica* survives at Chesterholm-*Vindolanda:* note the two steps to the left.

19. This figure of Mars originally stood over the entrance to the headquarters building at Housesteads.

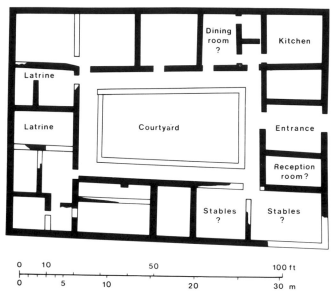

20. The commanding officer's house at Housesteads consists of a range of rooms round an open courtyard. It is unfortunate that in spite of excavation the function of many rooms is not known.

tion is not clear. At Housesteads in the fourth century weapons were stored in one of the rear rooms, possibly on an upper storey.

The cross-hall contained a tribunal at one end (see fig. 18). On this dais the commanding officer would stand to issue orders, probably including the orders for the day, hold courts martial and probably also dispense justice to the local civilians. In some forts it seems possible that most of the unit could have been assembled in the cross-hall. The orders for the day and other notices may have been posted here or on the courtyard verandah.

The front half of the headquarters was an open courtyard. A well generally lay within the court, which was surrounded by a verandah. Sometimes the verandah was enclosed, and the rooms thus created may have served as armouries. Although such rooms are known in the first century, they became more common in the third and fourth centuries when the verandahs were frequently completely closed in. At several forts in the mid second century granaries were inserted into the courtyard. In fourth-century Chesterholm the verandah appears to have served as a store, while at South Shields the cross-hall was converted to this purpose.

Across the front of some headquarters buildings lay another verandah. This feature is found from the first to the fourth centuries. In the late second or third centuries a different addition appears: a hall is occasionally built over the crossing of the *via praetoria* and *via principalis* in front of the headquarters.

The commanding officer's house followed the basic design of a house built in warmer climes: a range of rooms round an open courtyard (see fig. 20). Here was provided accommodation for the commanding officer, his family and his slaves: he might also have his own bath suite. Occasionally a second small court was attached to one side of the house: the function of this is not clear.

Granaries

Tacitus records that each fort should have food supplies to last a year, and indeed all forts were provided with granaries. In order to keep the food dry and fresh the floors of granaries were raised off the ground (see fig. 22). In a timber building this was achieved by supporting the floor on closely spaced posts. Often these posts were placed in trenches, thus providing the granary with its unique plan. The floor in a stone building was supported on stone pillars or low walls. The long external walls of granaries were

21. The timber granary erected at the Lunt, Baginton, in 1973. The loading bay allowed wagons to be backed up and unloaded under cover.

22. The northern of the pair of granaries at Housesteads looking south-east. The long side walls, unsupported by internal partitions, are buttressed externally. The entrance by the loading bay gave access to a raised timber floor supported on stone pillars.

supported by buttresses. These are sometimes explained as the support for heavy roofs of tiles or slates required to protect the building from fire arrows, or necessary to counterbalance the thrust of the grain, or to allow the intervening spaces to be louvred. However, it seems more probable that the buttresses were necessary to maintain walls not sustained by internal partitions. Louvred windows to aid ventilation are assumed. There was usually a wide entrance at one end of the granary, the external loading bay being protected sometimes by a porch. Nothing is known of the internal arrangements or the means used to store the food.

Hospital and workshop

The larger forts at least would have contained a hospital. This building, in plan, was a smaller version of the commanding officer's house, with the rooms ranged round a courtyard. The wards were generally separated by a small room, possibly a cupboard. A large room at one end is assumed to be an operating theatre.

Relatively little is known of the workshop, including whether or not there was one in every fort. Many workshops appear to be long buildings, with projecting wings at either end, or with the rooms arranged in two rows separated by a central corridor. Most items of military equipment, it seems, were provided by state factories, so presumably the workshops were mainly for the repair of damaged equipment.

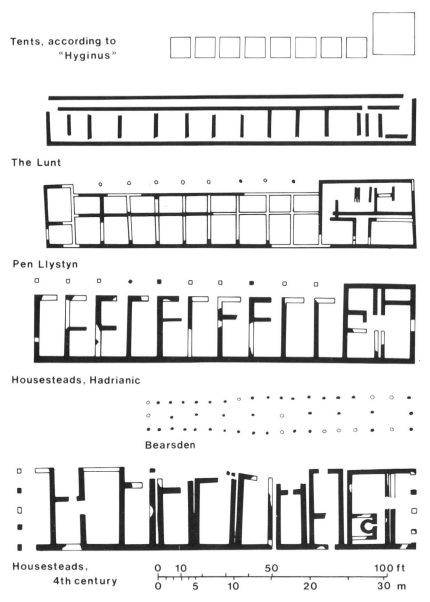

Tents, according to
"Hyginus"

The Lunt

Pen Llystyn

Housesteads, Hadrianic

Bearsden

Housesteads,
4th century

| 0 | 10 | 50 | 100 ft |
| 0 | 5 | 10 | 20 | 30 m |

23. Plans of barrack-blocks, with a century's row of tents drawn out for comparison. The Lunt was built in the 60s, Pen Llystyn about a decade later, Housesteads in the 120s, Bearsden in the 140s and the row of chalets at Housesteads in the fourth century. The row of tents and the barracks at the Lunt, Pen Llystyn and Housesteads appear to have been built for a century, while the barracks at Bearsden may have been designed for a cavalry troop.

Barrack-blocks

The barrack-block was a long building, being the descendant of the century's row of tents. At one end, usually by the rampart, lay the block for the centurion, while stretching away from this were ten small rooms, each probably for eight men as in the tent. Some early barrack-blocks contained only one room for each group of soldiers, and it was a small room too, being little larger than the 10 foot (3 m) square tent. But this is unusual and by the final decades of the first century it was normal for each barrack-room to be divided into a front room, presumably used for the storage of arms and equipment, and a rear room presumably for sleeping. (Nothing is known of sleeping arrangements, whether soldiers were in beds or bunks, or whether several soldiers slept in the same bed.) The rear room was usually somewhat larger than a tent.

Barrack-blocks with eight or nine rooms are generally considered to have been built for cavalry, two troops occupying each building, the soldiers being divided eight men to a room. In such barrack-blocks the front rooms are often larger than in infantry barracks, perhaps reflecting the greater space required for the trooper's equipment.

The stone barrack-blocks continued the arrangements of earlier years, at least into the third century. At the end of this century, or early in the fourth, fundamental changes occurred when the unitary barrack-block was replaced by a row of separate rooms or 'chalets'. The total floor area in a row of chalets was similar to that in its predecessor, but the different plan suggests a different organisation. That said, it is uncertain whether the army organisation had changed, there possibly being fewer men in each century, or whether soldiers' families were now allowed to live in the forts, one family perhaps occupying each chalet.

At some forts of the first and second centuries the barrack-blocks were divided into two (see fig. 33 for this arrangement in a fortlet). Occasionally barrack-blocks might, it seems, be divided longitudinally, the two halves being separated by a medial street, though how the soldiers were divided between the two buildings is not known.

Stables and storehouses

Very little is known about stables. The few excavated examples have been recognised by the occurrence of a drain, presumably for mucking out, running along the length of one wall.

Buildings would be required for the storage of arms and

24. A pair of barrack-blocks at Chesters looking towards the officers' blocks and the rampart. *(Above)* Reconstruction by M. J. Moore. *(Below)* The barrack-blocks as they are today. In the foreground two cavalry troopers stand talking, while on the verandah are two soldiers out of uniform.

25. The latrine at Housesteads. Wooden seating was placed over the main sewage conduit. The small channel on the central platform carried water used for the washing of the sponges used instead of toilet paper. The latrine was fed from water tanks, such as that visible.

armour, equipment such as tents, documents and records, and all the other paraphernalia required by an active army. Long narrow buildings appear in many forts and may have served this purpose.

Latrine and water supply

The communal latrine was normally placed against the rampart, on the lowest part of the fort. Where possible the latrine was flushed by water and the sewage carried away out of the fort (see fig. 25).

Many forts were provided with water tanks to collect rain water for use in flushing the latrines. Sometimes water filters enabled rain water to be used for drinking. Elsewhere aqueducts brought water into the fort: that at Greatchesters on Hadrian's Wall was 6 miles (10 km) long.

Bath-house

The bath-house was normally placed outside the fort, often in the annexe. Bath-houses, more than any other building, display considerable variation in their plans. The simple type consisted of a row of rooms extending from the changing room, through the cold room and one or two warm rooms, to the steam room by the furnace (see fig. 27). A refinement was to add a hot dry room to one side of the main range. One interesting group is the five bath-houses built to the same plan on the Hadrianic frontier. In these, the rooms providing the usual facilities were arranged in two rows, thus creating a compact building.

Bath-houses were provided with under-floor heating (hypocausts). The heat caused the soldiers to sweat: this, and the oil applied to the skin, brought out dirt from the pores, and all was scraped off with a blunt knife known as a *strigil*. After completing the heat treatment, the soldier would normally take a cold bath to

26. Reconstruction of the interior of the latrine at Bearsden, drawn by M. J. Moore.

close the pores before returning to the fort. It is not known how often soldiers bathed.

Annexe

Many forts had attached to them an annexe. This might contain timber or stone buildings providing extra storage, or facilities such as workshops, or the bath-house. The annexe would also

27. Plans of the bath-houses at Chesters on Hadrian's Wall and Bearsden on the Antonine Wall. The changing room and hot dry room at Chesters appear to be additions to the Hadrianic nucleus.

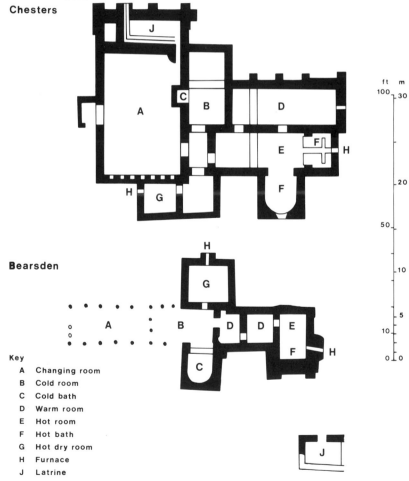

Chesters

Bearsden

Key

A	Changing room
B	Cold room
C	Cold bath
D	Warm room
E	Hot room
F	Hot bath
G	Hot dry room
H	Furnace
J	Latrine

28. The main spine of the bath-house at Bearsden runs east-west. The timber changing room (right) leads into the central hall or cold room. On the nearer side of this lies the hot dry room with its own furnace; to the left are the three rooms of the steam range, heated independently; beyond the cold room is the apsidal cold bath. The latrine is top left, while the buttresses of an earlier, unfinished bath-house are visible bottom left. (Crown Copyright.)

29. A reconstruction by M. J. Moore of the fort at Rough Castle on the Antonine Wall, viewed from the south-east. The ramparts are of turf and the gates of timber. Within the fort the principal buildings were of stone, the rest of timber. To the east lay a large annexe containing the garrison's bath-house: it is not known what happened in the rest of the annexe. The northern approach to the fort was protected by ten rows of defensive pits *(lilia)*.

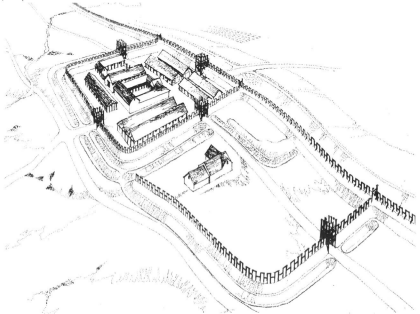

30. Hardknott looking east up the pass. The fort lies on the high ground immediately to the right of the crest of the ridge, with the parade ground beyond showing clearly as a square flat area somewhat larger than the fort.

afford protection for animals and wagons, goods in transit, or troops on the march. There is no clear evidence for its use by civilians.

The parade ground

The parade ground was placed adjacent to the fort (see fig. 30). It was simply a levelled area of ground, sometimes provided with a gravel surface, where parades could be held and training conducted. Here was a tribunal for the commanding officer and any other officers inspecting the troops. Here also was held the annual oath-taking, when a new altar was dedicated to Jupiter.

The Roman fort lacked certain buildings normally found in a

31. The legionary fortress at Inchtuthil, abandoned uncompleted probably in 86 or 87 (plan drawn by I. A. Richmond, but with additions). All the barrack-blocks had been completed but only six of the ten granaries. The barrack-blocks (e.g. 1) were arranged in cohorts, with the first cohort (2) situated in the place of honour to the right of the headquarters building (3): the houses for the centurions of the first cohort (e.g. 4) are larger than those for the other centurions (e.g. 5). The walls and raised floors of the granaries were supported on posts set in rows of parallel trenches (e.g. 6). The fort also contained a workshop (7) and a hospital (8). South of the *via principalis* lay several of the officers' houses (9), but others remained to be built. Small store rooms (e.g. 10) lay along the streets behind a colonnade.

INCHTUTHIL : GENERAL PLAN OF THE LEGIONARY FORTRESS

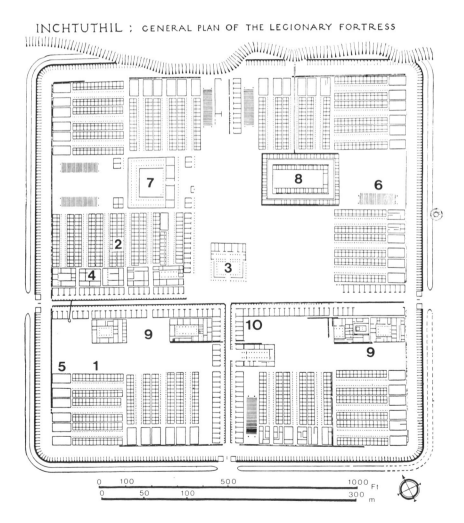

modern army camp. There were, for example, no communal messing facilities: it is presumed that soldiers normally ate in the front room of their barrack-blocks or on the verandah. Nor have ablutions blocks — for washing rather than bathing — been recognised in forts.

The fortress

At least ten legionary fortresses are known in Britain. Most lie under modern towns and have been only partly explored. However, one remains unencumbered by modern development and has been examined by means of selective trenching: Inchtuthil in Perthshire (fig. 31). The final report on the excavation of this site has not yet been published, so the following account is based on interim reports. The fortress was built in the decade 80-90, and probably in the years 85 and 86, and was abandoned unfinished. This single period fortress is one of the most important archaeological sites in Britain.

Inchtuthil was being constructed for a complete legion, possibly XX Valeria Victrix. It contained barrack accommodation for the ten cohorts of the legion, six barracks each for cohorts II to X, with special barracks next to the headquarters building for the first cohort. Each cohort had its own granary. Each senior officer in the legion had his own house, though not all had been built when the fortress was abandoned, and in addition there were a hospital and a workshop. Spaces were left for the legate's house and other general buildings. The bath-house lay outside the fortress but had not been used when demolished.

With the exception of the bath-house and the fort wall the whole of Inchtuthil was built in timber. Its construction may have taken two years, possibly longer, and special temporary 'labour' camps were built for the soldiers while they worked on the fortress. During this time the soldiers seem to have lived in tents, while some officers and stores appear to have been housed in wooden buildings.

The fortress was carefully demolished by the army on its abandonment. The buildings were knocked down, surplus stores buried — about one million nails were disposed of in this way — pottery and glass smashed. The site was indeed left as a desert.

In broad outline the other legionary fortresses were similar to Inchtuthil. Perhaps the most interesting additional information comes from Caerleon in South Wales, where an amphitheatre, no doubt for training purposes, has been found immediately outside the fortress wall (fig. 32).

32. The amphitheatre at Caerleon lay just outside the walls of the legionary fortress. (Crown Copyright.)

The fortlet

In many instances the army required to outpost a group of soldiers to guard a river crossing or a road, or to maintain surveillance over a certain point. In such circumstances a detachment would be sent out from a nearby auxiliary unit. The detachment might consist of a complete century or might be made up of men drawn from different centuries and troops. Documentary sources indicate that such detachments might be outposted for several years. Fortlets to house such groups are attested in Britain from soon after the conquest into the fourth century. An early example is at Martinhoe, on the north Devon

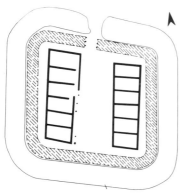

33. The second-century fortlet at Barburgh Mill contained two barrack-blocks, together of a size to accommodate a century. The timber barrack-blocks were protected by a turf rampart and a single ditch.

34 *(below)*. A reconstruction of the fortlet at Barburgh Mill by M. J. Moore.

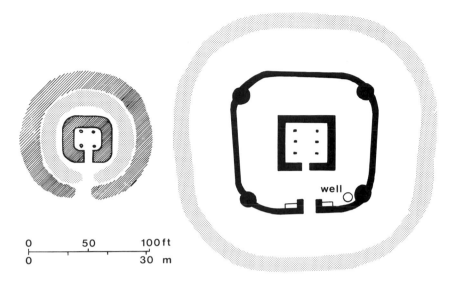

0   50   100 ft

0   30   m

35. The watch-towers at Parkneuk on the Gask Ridge (left) and at Goldsborough. The tower at Parkneuk, built in the late first century, was of timber and was protected by a turf rampart within a single ditch: upcast from the ditch was thrown out on to the outer lip. At Goldsborough the late fourth-century tower was of stone, as was the perimeter wall: beyond lay a ditch.

36. A reconstruction by M. J. Moore of the tower at Parkneuk on the Gask Ridge, probably built in the 80s.

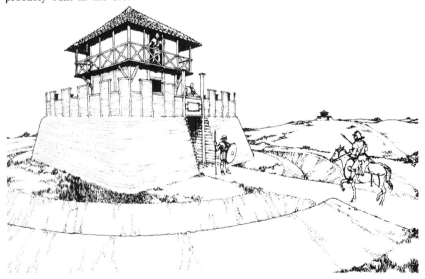

coast, where the purpose of the detachment appears to have been to observe the Bristol Channel. Three small timber buildings provided accommodation for an officer and perhaps eighty men — a century.

In the second century several fortlets were built in southern Scotland during the Antonine occupation (about 140-63). One example, at Barburgh Mill, has been completely excavated and found to contain two buildings (see figs. 33 and 34). Together these buildings contained an officer's suite and ten rooms, the normal accommodation of a century.

The milecastles and milefortlets of the Hadrianic frontier and the fortlets of the Antonine Wall are, essentially, smaller versions of these fortlets. Those on Hadrian's Wall appear to provide accommodation either for eight men or thirty-two men, charged with the tasks of guarding the gate through the Wall at the milecastle and observing their section of the barrier.

The tower

The Roman army constructed towers for signalling and observation. Much has been written on Roman signal-stations and methods of communication, but little can be proved. Chains of closely spaced towers for observation of the frontier first appear in the late first century in Britain and Germany. In Britain it seems possible that the towers along the road running north from Ardoch to Bertha in Perthshire were constructed in the years following the abandonment of Inchtuthil, about 87-90. The closeness of the towers — from half a mile to a mile (0.8 to 1.6 km) apart — emphasises that the occupants were not concerned with sending messages, but with the observation of the movement of people across the frontier line.

Towers in the first century were of timber (see figs. 35 and 36). Four large posts usually provided the framework for the tower, which was defended by a rampart and ditch. In the first half of the second century, stone came to be used in towers, certainly in the precursors of Hadrian's Wall in Cumbria and on the Wall itself, where even the towers in the turf section of the Wall were of stone. In the late fourth century a series of stone towers was constructed along the cliffs of the Yorkshire coast, presumably to help survey the sea for invaders or pirates. These towers are similar to those of the second century, though in detail they differ for the walls of the towers are more massive, suggesting a higher structure, while the turf rampart has also been replaced by a stone wall.

5
Building the fort

The Roman army contained its own building and maintenance staff. Each legion carried on its strength surveyors, architect-engineers, masons, carpenters, glaziers and so on. Although all such building work was at first carried out by the legionaries, who constructed both Hadrian's Wall and the Antonine Wall for example, from the second century the auxiliary units probably contained their own small building staffs. While skilled craftsmen planned and erected the buildings, the fetching and carrying was done by other soldiers.

The first step in building a fort was to choose its location. Generally, a low flat-topped hill or elevated platform was chosen. This would aid defence, while allowing wide views. Defence was not paramount and sites with steep sides were not used, for these would offer no advantage to an offensive army. A water supply was important and therefore most forts lay beside a river or stream. No doubt on occasions the governor himself would choose the site of the fort, though this task may also have fallen to the legionary camp prefects, whose responsibility included the artisans of the unit: in AD 50, for example, a camp prefect was in charge of troops building forts in South Wales.

In order to protect themselves while constructing the fort, the builders in many instances threw up a temporary or labour camp. Several of these have been recognised outside forts in Scotland, including Inchtuthil. Many forts, it may be suspected, were built in partially cleared countryside. Trees and other vegetation would be removed from the site of the fort, good timber presumably being stored for later use: seasoned timber was not required so recently felled material would be of value. An area much larger than the fort itself would be stripped to allow for the defences and a cleared area around. A fort with an internal area of 4 acres (1.6 ha) might require 14 acres (5.7 ha) to be cleared. The surveyor would have then laid out the plan of the fort. A cross-staff *(groma)* allowed right angles to be achieved, while lengths were measured by marked staffs.

The order of works thereafter is not known. On Trajan's Column soldiers are shown working on the defences and the interior at the same time. In preparation for their excavation, the ditches may have been first marked out by a small trench. Turf stripped from their surface and the surface of the fort would presumably have been used in the rampart if suitable: care was taken to obtain the best turf so this might entail ranging further afield than the immediate site. Local timber, wherever possible, was cut for the buildings. Oak was specially favoured for its durable qualities, but when that was not available other timber was used: alder, ash, birch or elm. Smaller branches would be required for the wattle and daub walls of timber buildings: willow was preferred, but alder and hazel were also used. In total, perhaps between 16 and 30 acres (6.5 to 12.1 ha) of woodland might be required to provide the timber for a 4 acre (1.6 ha) fort.

There is no evidence that the army had dumps of timber ready for the construction of new forts, or that buildings were prefabricated. Rather, local resources were tapped. But, while turf, timber, clay and stone might have been available locally, other items, such as nails and glass, would have to be imported. Large quantities of nails in particular would have been required for the construction of forts, and the one million dumped at Inchtuthil when the fortress was abandoned indicate the numbers involved.

37. On this scene from Trajan's Column legionaries are constructing a turf rampart. Each block of turf is carried on the shoulders of a soldier, held on by a short length of rope. In the foreground a ditch is being dug. The earth is being removed in wicker baskets.

38. This inscription records the construction *(FECIT)* of one of the buildings in the fort at Bearsden on the Antonine Wall by legion XX Valeria Victrix *(LEG XX V V)* under the command of an officer whose name has been shortened to *QUINT.* (Crown Copyright.)

Sizes were, to some extent, standardised. Measurements might be laid down in the manual; for example, the fourth-century writer Vegetius states that a turf should measure 18 by 12 by 6 inches (450 by 300 by 150 mm). Experience in building also no doubt led to a certain amount of uniformity. In the first century gateposts were normally 10 to 12 inches (250 to 300 mm) across, while in the second century they tended to measure about 9 inches (230 mm) or a little less. The main uprights in the internal buildings were slighter, normally about 3-4 inches (75 to 100 mm) across, while the wattles, thin branches, were a mere half an inch (13 mm) or less in diameter. The size of timbers used suggests that the buildings would be single-storey, though there is a hint at two-storey buildings on Trajan's Column. Internally the buildings were probably normally plastered and painted, and sometimes externally also. Windows were closed by wooden shutters: the evidence for window glass in association with timber buildings is slight. The roofs were usually thatched or shingled, though occasionally tiles or slates were used. Floors were frequently of gravel or beaten clay.

Building in stone led to a requirement not only for good building stone such as sandstone or limestone, but also for limestone for mortar, sand and copious quantities of water. Not all stone buildings were roofed in tile or slate; sometimes thatch

39. This scene from Trajan's Column shows legionary carpenters at work on the gates to left and right, ditch diggers in the foreground filling their baskets with earth, and the rampart builders in the background. Beside the ditch (right) a soldier attends to a catapult pulled by a mule, while a group of auxiliaries approaches from the left.

or shingle continued to be used. Again local sources were tapped wherever possible, as the line of quarries along Hadrian's Wall bears out. Other items, such as tiles, might be specially manufactured by the army.

Stone building inscriptions provide a rare insight into the construction of buildings, and indeed also of larger undertakings such as Hadrian's Wall. The discovery of brief inscriptions recording the activities of different building gangs demonstrates that the gangs were expected to 'sign' their work, thus rendering it available for inspection (see fig. 38). It seems that these gangs normally worked under the command of their centurion.

The tools the soldiers used would have included axes for tree felling. One useful implement, the *dolabra,* had an axe on one end of the head and an adze or a point on the other. For digging, a sort of entrenching tool was used: spades and shovels were also used by the Romans but are rarely found in military contexts. Baskets were used to move earth. Turf cutters are known, and turves were carried on the shoulders, held on by a short length of rope, which is one of the items listed by Josephus as required by every soldier. This list includes a chain and a saw, obviously important in clearing ground. Scythes were also supplied for cutting grass.

40. These carpenter's tools from the fort at Newstead include (from top left to bottom right) axe, auger, chisel, compasses, file, saw and two plane blades.

Carpenters and smiths needed special tools (see fig. 40). The fort at Newstead in the Borders furnished a wide range of tools used by both. Hammers, chisels, mallets, planes, files and augers were all in the tool box of the carpenter, while the smith carried hammer, tongs, anvil etc.

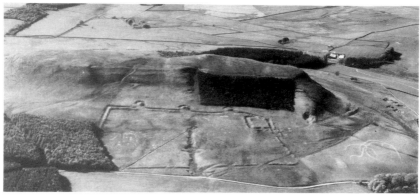

41. Burnswark in Dumfriesshire was probably a training area for the Roman army stationed on the northern frontier. Semi-permanent camps lie on either side of the abandoned hillfort. The south camp lies in the foreground, with the earlier second-century fortlet at its north-east corner.

42. The temple of Mithras at Carrawburgh lies beyond the south-west corner of the fort (visible top right). Benches flanked a nave leading to three altars dedicated by prefects of the local unit. The roof was supported by timber uprights, here shown as stumps.

6
Life in the fort

The title of this chapter is in many ways a misnomer. The fort was merely the base of the soldiers stationed there. In the summer most would have been out training, building practice camps, engaging in manoeuvres, chasing brigands, patrolling, supervising frontier tribes or the mines, collecting food, clothing, arms, armour or horses, perhaps even fighting. Nevertheless, some soldiers would have stayed at base, and daily routine would have continued. Many documents illustrate these facets of military life. Most of these records were found in the deserts of Syria or Egypt, but military records written on wooden tablets have been recovered from Chesterholm-*Vindolanda*.

The official day started with the morning report. This was written and included the date; the name of the unit; the number of men and officers in the unit; the name of the commanding officer; the password; departures and returns and other items of business; the orders of the day; the soldiers on guard duty that day. Passwords were, for example, 'Security', 'Jupiter Dolichenus *sanctus*', 'Mercury *sanctus*'. The only recorded guard duty in the morning report was that at the standards, where about ten men under the command of a centurion or decurion were posted. These soldiers guarded the *aedes* and presumably also the entrance to the headquarters building. Although not detailed in the morning report, guards were also posted, day and night, at the gates, on the ramparts and at key points in the fort such as the granary, while there were also mobile patrols. Guards might also be posted at important points outside the fort.

The soldiers working in the rooms at the rear of the headquarters prepared the morning report and other documents. Duty rosters covered ten days or more and the duties included cleaning uniform, latrine fatigues, headquarters guard, gate guard and escort. Each soldier had his own file, on which were recorded details relating to his enlistment, his duties, and other relevant information. At least once a year a report of the strength of each unit was prepared and sent to provincial headquarters, presumably for onward transmission to Rome. In addition there were accounts, orders, receipts, records of materials and horses, pay records, savings records, letters and so on.

All documents were prepared by clerks, who received no extra pay but had immunity from general fatigues. Such soldiers were called *immunes,* and this category also included smiths, carpenters, builders, armourers, medical orderlies and musicians (for calling out the watch and orders in battle, not for playing in the regimental band, though they did take part in official functions, for example religious ceremonies).

Josephus remarked that the Roman army was so well trained that its exercises were bloodless battles and its battles bloody exercises. Vegetius, writing over two hundred years later, recorded that all soldiers were to undergo weapons training each morning on the parade ground (see fig. 30), in the drill hall or in the amphitheatre (see fig. 32). This training was not restricted to weapons drill but included physical training, swimming, military exercises and manoeuvres. The cavalry exercises could be particularly impressive and included mock fights between Greeks and Amazons. Another important activity was the construction of practice camps: sometimes these camps might then be used for mock battles. In north Britain one such area seems to have been used on more than one occasion: the practice camps on either side of Burnswark Hill in Dumfriesshire may have been a training area for the army of the north (see fig. 41).

In addition to these duties there were general fatigues to be endured. The fort had to be kept tidy; armour and equipment had to be cleaned and polished; firewood and water required collection; the latrines needed to be cleaned out. And in cavalry units horses had to be groomed, fed and watered, while the stables had to be mucked out.

The preparation of food and eating would have taken up some of the soldiers' time each day. Records show that they had a varied diet. Corn was the staple food and could be used to make bread or a kind of porridge. Meat of some variety was also consumed: beef, mutton, ham, veal and poultry were all eaten. Fruit included blackberries, strawberries, bilberries and cherries while vegetables and nuts were also eaten. Both beer and wine were drunk. There were fixed times for the meals, which were probably a light breakfast and a main meal in the evening. While in theory each soldier was issued with his own food from the granaries, it seems probable that those soldiers in each barrack room who were off-duty cooked for those on duty. The cooking was carried out in hearths and ovens set into the rear of the ramparts. There were no communal messes in Roman forts so it seems probable that the troops either ate in the open or in their barrack-rooms.

Old Carlisle

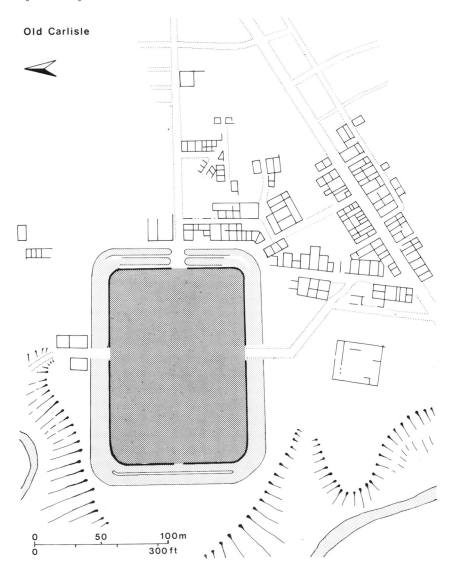

43. The fort and civil settlement at Old Carlisle in Cumbria, drawn from aerial photographs (after Salway).

44. The fort and civil settlement at Chesterholm-*Vindolanda* looking south. The headquarters building lies in the centre of the fort. The civil settlement straddles the road leading out of the west gate of the fort. Top right stand the modern reconstructions of Hadrian's Wall.

It is not known how much free time was allowed to the soldiers. There were no such things as weekends or forty-eight hour passes. Leave had to be applied for to the centurion, and it is clear that bribes helped. Off duty at the fort, the soldier could gamble with his colleagues. Gaming boards and dice have been found at forts. One game was known as the *ludus latrunculorum:* it was a kind of soldiers' war game. The bath-house was available, though it is not known how frequently it was used by the soldiers (see figs. 27 and 28). Outside the fort there lay delights in the civil settlement (see figs. 43 and 44). Here were taverns, shops, gambling dens, brothels and entertainment for the soldiers, all provided by people whose main aim was to relieve them of as much money as possible, as well as temples (see fig. 42) and the houses of soldiers' families. Such villages sprang up outside most Roman forts: indeed merchants might follow the army on campaign and erect their booths outside the camp rampart. Sometimes the village acquired its own vitality and when the army moved on, abandoning the fort, it survived and prospered; many towns in southern Britain started their lives as civil settlements outside forts. In the north, though, these villages were patently an artificial creation, dependent upon the army for their existence, and they did not survive the end of Roman rule in Britain.

Roman soldiers were not allowed to marry according to Roman law, but they were permitted to contract unions following local custom, and it is clear that many soldiers did. Some time must therefore have been spent with the family in the settlement outside the fort. On retirement, too, the soldier would generally have stayed here. The soldiers' families in the villages outside forts were a useful source of recruits to the army. Within a little over a generation from AD 43 the Roman army had begun to accept recruits from the British tribes. Some soldiers entered units stationed in Britain, others were formed into regiments and posted abroad. The proportion of men of British birth serving in the army in Britain steadily increased so that by the second half of the second century most of the units in Britain, although bearing foreign titles, were made up predominantly of local men. This situation obtained until the fall of the empire, though re-inforcements from the continent were occasionally posted to the island. The sons of soldiers, living in the villages outside forts, mostly followed their fathers into the 'family regiment'.

The soldiers might own slaves. Slaves might be distributed as booty following a campaign: Caesar gave one slave to each soldier following a victorious battle in Gaul. Inscriptions from Britain attest that soldiers owned slaves, who might even have gone into business on their master's behalf. Where these slaves lived and slept is a matter of conjecture.

The routine of military life was broken by various events. There were frequent religious ceremonies. The main ceremonies involved the whole unit and included the sacrifice of animals. Three times, later four times, a year the unit assembled for the pay parade. The first was held on 1st January, when each unit in the army paraded to swear the oath of allegiance to the emperor and receive the first of three (later four) annual pay instalments. Part of the pay was deducted for food, bedding, clothing and the annual camp dinner. As inflation ate into the value of money in the fourth century, more came to be provided in kind.

At certain times there might be special parades or inspections. Each governor normally toured his command on taking up his appointment, preparing a report for the emperor. Sometimes the emperor himself might order such a parade, as Hadrian did in 128 when in north Africa. Part of the address he made to the units inspected on that tour still survives.

While Trajan inveighed against the troops being away from the colours, it is clear from surviving military documents that many soldiers spent long periods away from their fort. Some served on outpost duty. Records from Syria demonstrate that soldiers were frequently away for three years or more at outposts up to 150 miles (240 km) distant from the parent fort. Some stores were delivered to the fort, but others were collected. In 105 soldiers from a unit based in Macedonia were in Gaul collecting clothing, a journey which must have taken several weeks.

Craftsmen and technicians might be outposted to special works depots: the Twentieth Legion had a tilery at Holt, 8 miles (13 km) south of its fortress at Chester, while in the third and fourth centuries, soldiers from legions II and XX outstationed at Corbridge were engaged in industrial activity, possibly the manufacture of weapons.

Soldiers might serve for a number of years at provincial headquarters, for the governor and his senior officers drew their staffs from the units under his command. As there was no police force in the Roman empire, soldiers were also called upon to fulfil that role. Thus they were employed to chase brigands or apprehend criminals. Crowd control and the suppression of riots fell to the army, and even the search for missing persons. The judiciary called upon the army too: the escort of prisoners, guard duty at the courts and the execution of the sentence all devolved upon the army. Convicts were sometimes sent to the mines, and this was partly the reason for the involvement of troops with these. In Britain there is evidence for soldiers associated with the mining of lead, silver, iron and gold, as well as coal. The collection of taxes could also be a military function. In frontier areas soldiers might take on the collection of customs duties and the supervision of local markets, especially those which might be attended by people from outside the province. Finally, army specialists were sometimes lent to civilians to aid in their projects, normally civil engineering works. There was undoubtedly much to take the soldier away from his fort.

Under siege

There are no descriptions of Roman forts in Britain being attacked, though brief references to camps and building parties, forts and frontiers being assailed do survive. The night attack on the camp of the Ninth Legion in 81 or 82 demonstrates the importance and efficacy of such temporary defensive measures, for the legion would almost certainly have been overwhelmed by the Caledonians if it had not been protected by the defences of the temporary camp. The defences of the fort were more formidable, with a higher rampart and a greater number of ditches: they must have presented a daunting obstacle to an enemy not equipped for siege warfare. Yet their defences were fairly slight when compared to contemporary town walls or later military enclosures. They reflect the fact that at this time the Roman army was essentially an offensive, not a defensive, force.

The provision of weapons was another reflection of the role of the army, for it was ill equipped to fight a siege. Soldiers might be trained in archery, according to writers of the second and fourth centuries AD, but the bow does not appear to have been a normal piece of military equipment. Cicero, under attack in camp in Gaul, used specially prepared siege spears and sharpened stakes, while one of his colleagues in similar circumstances found the artillery (arrow and stone firing catapults) of great value. Trajan's Column reveals Roman soldiers throwing turves at their attackers!

The relatively slight defences of the camp or fort might be rushed, but in the later empire that problem was overcome by the construction of high walls, impossible to breach by an army lacking siege machinery. Sometimes special platforms might be constructed on or by the fort walls for the artillery but little is known about these. The only recognised examples lie at High Rochester, where such platforms were constructed and repaired in the 220s. The platforms were probably intended for the *onager,* the one-armed stone-throwing machine. The provision of such machines does not appear to be normal and is probably an extra defensive measure at this fort.

The enemy did sometimes penetrate the Roman defences, though the scant literary sources for Roman Britain usually imply that the barbarians preferred to avoid Roman forts, leaving the garrisons isolated, than to waste time in capturing them. However, a fourth-century tombstone from Ambleside records the death of a fifty-five year-old retired centurion and his son, an army records officer aged thirty-five, killed in the fort by the enemy. It is unfortunate that nothing is known of the occasion of this attack.

Tacitus records an important precaution against capitulation during siege: the provision of adequate supplies. The details are lost, but forts were clearly provisioned so that, if necessary, they could survive the winter months without further supplies of food.

45. The earthworks of the fort at Ardoch are the best preserved in Britain. They reflect the complex history of the site, the fort apparently contracting within two outer ditches so that the mid second-century fort was protected by five ditches on both the east and north sides. (Crown Copyright.)

Demolition

Buildings do not last for ever but have to be frequently repaired and replaced. Timber buildings in particular are subject to decay. Many of the earlier forts in Britain, therefore, reveal evidence for several phases of rebuilding within a comparatively short time, though such rebuilding may reflect the transitory nature of the garrison, as well as the materials of construction. Indeed there is a hint from some sites that when the garrison changed, the fort — or perhaps just the barrack accommodation — was demolished in preparation for rebuilding by the new unit.

Abandonment of a fort also led to demolition. The army seems to have demolished the buildings, burning the combustible material on site. Sometimes timbers were uprooted, sometimes they were left standing charred and half burned. Stone buildings were unroofed but there is little evidence to suggest that they were systematically demolished. Rarely, however, was much attention paid to the defences: probably the breastwork was usually pulled down; the ditches were mostly left open. It is doubtful if the army salvaged much building material for use elsewhere. It was usually easier to make anew than to carry building materials, at great trouble and expense, over considerable distances. Thus about a million nails were buried at Inchtuthil when the fortress was abandoned in or shortly after 86 while glass and pottery were smashed and dumped in drains and gullies. Other items were also buried. Care seems to have been taken with altars and other inscriptions. The distance slabs on the Antonine Wall all seem to have been removed from their bases and carefully buried faced downwards when the Wall was abandoned, while at Bar Hill the unit's altars were dropped into the well. These objects — ironwork and dedications — were items to be placed out of reach of the barbarians.

The end of Roman rule in Britain led to the dispersal of the army, but not necessarily the end of their buildings. There was no attempt to demolish forts, as the remains such as Portchester and Pevensey demonstrate. The perimeter walls of these Saxon Shore forts survived to be reused as castles in the middle ages. Recent work has demonstrated that the headquarters building at York survived into the ninth century before its enormous columns came crashing down. Many forts served more peaceful purposes in their later days for they attracted early missionaries who built their churches over the abandoned military remains. Thus it came about that the Roman army was replaced by the Roman church.

46. The fort at Caernarfon lies in the centre of the modern town. Visible on this aerial photograph is the full circuit of the defences, the headquarters building (partially overlain by modern houses), the commanding officer's house to the left, and barrack-blocks, storehouses and workshops beyond. Excavations are taking place in the *praetentura* in the foreground.

7
Select gazetteer

Fragments of many Roman forts survive in Britain. The following list is not intended to be exhaustive, but to indicate briefly the main visible forts, fortlets, watch-towers and camps and their main features. For further information, including access directions, the reader is directed to Roger J. A. Wilson, *A Guide to the Roman Remains in Britain* (1980) and David E. Johnston (editor), *Discovering Roman Britain* (Shire Publications, 1983). An asterisk marks those sites which are open to the public. At other sites the owner should be consulted before entering his land. The National Grid Reference is given immediately after the name of the site.

SCOTLAND

Inchtuthil legionary fortress (NO 125396). Denuded remains of the defences intermittently visible (see fig. 31).

*****Ardoch** fort, annexe, camps (NN 840100). The earthen defences of the fort are remarkably well preserved. Two stretches of the 130 acre (53 ha) camp defences survive, including an entrance (see fig. 45).

The Antonine Wall

*****Rough Castle** fort (NS 843798). A small fort attached to the Antonine Wall: turf ramparts, ditches, defensive pits *(lilia)*, annexe visible (see fig. 29).

*****Bar Hill** fort (NS 707759). Fragments of headquarters building and bath-house visible.

*****Bearsden** bath-house (NS 545721). (See figs. 12, 27 and 28.)

*****Kinneil** fortlet (NS 977803). Remains of turf ramparts; wooden posts mark the position of the timber buildings.

*****Cramond** fort (NT 189769). Headquarters building, granaries, workshop, together with other buildings, restored in outline.

Many site are visible as earthworks.

Camps: **Raedykes** (NO 842902), **Kirkbuddo** (NO 494440) (fig. 4), **Pennymuir** (NT 754140) (fig. 2).
   Burnswark (NY 185787). Two camps on either side of an abandoned iron age hillfort — probably an army training area; the south camp has an earlier fortlet in one corner (fig. 41).

Forts: **Lyne** (NT 187405) and **Birrens** (NY 218752).

Fortlets: **Durisdeer** (NS 902048), **Castle Creg** (NT 050592),
   Redshaw Burn (NT 030139), **Kaimes Castle** (NN 861129),
   Outerwards (NS 232666), and **Lurg Moor** (NS 295737).
Watch-towers: **Parkneuk** (NN 916184) (figs. 35 and 36), *****Muir
   O'Fauld (NN 981189) and **Brownhart Law** (NT 790096).

NORTHERN ENGLAND

*****South Shields** fort (NZ 365677). A supply base in the early third
   century; several granaries are visible (overlying earlier workshop and barrack-blocks), headquarters building with strongroom, water settling tanks, and defences (fig. 5). In 1986 the
   west gate was rebuilt (see fig. 47).

Hadrian's Wall
*****Chesters** fort (NY 913701). Walls, headquarters building,
   commanding officer's house, barrack-blocks and bath-house
   visible (figs. 16, 24 and 27).
*****Housesteads** fort (NY 790687). Walls, headquarters building,
   commanding officer's house, granaries, hospital, latrines and
   fourth-century barrack-blocks visible. Also several houses in
   the civil settlement (see figs. 1, 13, 15, 19, 20, 22, 23 and 25).
*****Chesterholm-***Vindolanda** (NY 771664). Fort with wall and
   headquarters building, bath-house and extensive civil settlement (see figs. 17, 18 and 44).

*****Corbridge** military compounds (NY 983649). Third and fourth-
   century legionary compounds with headquarters buildings (one
   with strongroom), workshops and officers' houses. Also visible
   are two granaries, an aqueduct and parts of the earlier forts: a
   headquarters building and commanding officer's house.
*****Hardknott** fort (NY 218015). Second-century fort in beautiful
   country. Fort wall, headquarters building, commanding officer's house, granaries, bath-house, and, most importantly,
   parade ground (see fig. 30).
*****Ambleside** fort (NY 372039). Second-century fort with gates,
   headquarters building, commanding officer's house, granaries,
   all in dilapidated condition.
*****Ravenglass** bath-house (SD 086962). Highest standing walls of a
   bath-house in Britain, but not readily intelligible.
Whitley Castle fort (NY 690480). Earthworks of defences very
   well preserved.
Ebchester fort (NZ 102556). Part of the commanding officer's
   bath-house.

*Binchester fort (NZ 210314). Very well preserved remains of the fourth-century commanding officer's bath-house.
*Ribchester fort (SD 650350). Parts of two granaries.
*York legionary fortress (SE 600520). Parts of the walls visible, in particular the multangular tower; remains of internal buildings in Minster undercroft, particularly the headquarters.
*Chester legionary fortress (SJ 405664). Some sections of walls visible and amphitheatre.
The fort platform and ditches remain visible at several sites: **Risingham** (NY 890862), *Carrawburgh (NY 859713) (see fig. 42 for Mithraeum outside fort), **Maryport** (NY 030370), **Old Carlisle** (NY 260460), **Brougham** (NY 530280), **Brough under Stainmore** (NY 790140), **Greta Bridge** (NZ 085132), **Low Burrow Bridge** (NY 600010), **Lanchester** (NZ 160469). The complete circuit of the stone wall, together with four gates, can be seen at *Birdoswald (NY 615663), while two gates are visible at **High Rochester** (NY 830980).
At **Chew Green** (NT 780080) there is a fortlet and several camps (see fig. 4), and at **Cawthorn** (SE 780900) a fort and three camps. There is a well preserved marching camp at **Four Laws** (NY 905825) while a first-century camp may be inspected at **Reycross** (NY 900123) (see fig. 4), and a fortlet at **Maiden Castle** (NY 873130), 2 miles (3 km) to the west. On *Hadrian's Wall many milecastles (e.g. 37, 42, 48 and 49) and turrets (e.g. 7b, 26b, 33b, 41a, 51a, 51b and 52a) can be visited. On **Bowes Moor** (NY 929125) the turf rampart of a signal-station survives and at *Scarborough (TA 050893) the lines of the stone fourth-century watch-tower have been picked out in modern stones (see fig. 35).

MIDLANDS

*The Lunt, Baginton fort (SP 344752). This fort has been completely excavated and a timber gate, together with the adjoining stretch of rampart, and a timber granary have been restored (see cover and figs. 7, 21 and 23).

WALES

*Caernarfon fort (SH 485624). Parts of the stone wall and stone gates are visible, as is the headquarters building, with a strongroom, commanding officer's house and workshop. Here also is the enclosure known as Hen Waliau, possibly a stores compound, with walls up to 18 feet (5.5 m) high, surviving in private gardens.

Caer Gybi (SH 248826). A three-sided enclosure, probably a landing place dating to the late third or fourth centuries.

Tomen-y-Mur fort (SH 707388). The earthworks of this two-period fort survive, overlain by a Norman motte. Also the parade ground, a probable amphitheatre, and a practice camp.

*Brecon Gaer fort (SO 003296). Sections of stone wall and gates visible.

*Caerleon fortress (ST 338903). Open to visitors are part of the stone wall, a barrack-block (with an additional three laid out in plan using modern stones), latrine, part of a bath-house, and, outside the fortress, the amphitheatre (see fig. 32).

*Cardiff fort (ST 181766). Rebuilt, on Roman foundations, in the nineteenth century, this reconstruction gives a splendid impression of what a late Roman fort might have looked like (see fig. 14).

*Y Pigwn camps (SN 827313). Two marching camps, one inside the other.

Other forts survive as earthworks: **Gaer Gae** (SH 878315), **Castell Collen** (SO 055628), **Coelbren** (SN 859107), **Gelligaer** (ST 133973). At **Neath** (SS 748977) two stone gateways have been preserved.

SOUTH-WEST ENGLAND

Martinhoe (SS 660490) and **Old Burrow** (SS 788493) fortlets both survive as earthworks.

Hod Hill fort (ST 857106). The earthworks of the mid first-century Roman fort placed in the corner of an iron age fort (see fig. 6).

SAXON SHORE FORTS

*Burgh Castle (TG 475046). Three walls survive, 20 feet (6 m) high, with external bastions, and a gate.

*Reculver (TR 227692). Most of two of the fort walls are visible, and two gates, though badly robbed.

*Richborough (TR 327602). A short section of the twin ditches of the Claudian base and the triple ditches of the third-century fort are visible within the massive late third-century wall and its double ditches, together with remains of other dates.

Lympne (TR 110340). Some sections of the fort wall remain, though badly disturbed by landslips.

*Pevensey (TQ 645048). Most of the wall of this oval fort survives, with bastions and two gates (see fig. 11).

*Portchester (SU 625046). Exceptionally well preserved fort wall with bastions, and four gates (see fig. 10).

47. The west gate of the fort at South Shields, rebuilt in 1986.

8
Further reading

Camps
Maxwell, G. S. 'Agricola's Campaigns: The Evidence of the Temporary Camps.' *Scottish Archaeological Forum* 12 (1981) 25-54.
St Joseph, J. K. S. 'Air Reconnaissance of Roman Scotland, 1939-75.' *Glasgow Archaeological Journal* 4 (1976) 1-28.
Wilson, D. R. 'Air Reconnaissance and Roman Military Antiquities in Britain.' *Scottish Archaeological Forum* 7 (1976) 13-30.

Forts
Breeze, D. J., and Dobson, B. 'Fort Types on Hadrian's Wall.' *Archaeologia Aeliana* 4 series, 47 (1969) 15-32.
Collingwood, R. G., and Richmond, I. A. *The Archaeology of Roman Britain.* 1969. (Chapters II-V.)
Johnson, Anne. *Roman Forts.* 1983.
Wilson, R. J. A. *Roman Forts: An Illustrated Introduction to the Garrison Posts of Roman Britain.* 1980.

Wales
Nash-Williams, V. E. *The Roman Frontier in Wales.* Second edition revised by M. G. Jarrett, 1969.

Northern England
Breeze, D. J., and Dobson, B. *Hadrian's Wall.* Third edition, 1987.
Bruce, J. C. *Handbook to the Roman Wall.* Thirteenth edition revised by C. M. Daniels, 1979.

Scotland
Hanson, W. S., and Maxwell, G. S. *Rome's North-west Frontier: The Antonine Wall.* 1983; paperback 1986.
Keppie, L. J. F. *Scotland's Roman Remains,* 1986.

The Saxon Shore
Johnson, J. S. *Roman Forts of the Saxon Shore.* Revised edition, 1979.
Johnson, J. S. *Late Roman Fortifications.* 1983.
Maxfield, V. A. (editor). *The Saxon Shore.* 1989.

Individual buildings
Davidson, D. P. *The Barracks of the Roman Army from the 1st to 3rd Centuries AD.* British Archaeological Reports, International Series 472, 1989.

Jones, M. J. *Roman Fort-Defences to AD 117.* British Archaeological Reports 21, 1978.
Manning, W. H., and Scott, I. R. 'Roman Timber Military Gaeways.' *Britannia* 10 (1979) 19-61.
Gentry, A. P. *Roman Military Stone-built Granaries in Britain.* British Archaeological Reports 32, 1976.
Manning, W. H. 'Roman Military Timber Granaries in Britain.' *Saalburg Jahrbuch* 32 (1975) 105-29.
Rickman, G. E. *Roman Granaries and Store Buildings.* 1971.
Welsby, D. A. *The Roman Military Defence of the British Provinces in Its Later Phases.* British Archaeological Reports 101, 1982.

Fortresses
Boon, G. C. *The Legionary Fortress of Caerleon-Isca.* 1987.
Petrikovits, H. von. *Die Innenbauten römischer Legionslager während der Principatszeit.* 1975.
Webster, G. (editor). *Fortress into City.* 1988.

Fortlets
Breeze, D. J. 'The Roman Fortlet at Barburgh Mill, Dumfriesshire.' *Britannia* 5 (1974) 130-62.

Building
Hanson, W. S. 'The Organisation of Roman Military Timber-Supply.' *Britannia* 9 (1978) 293-305.
Hanson, W. S. 'Military Timber Buildings: Construction and Reconstruction' in S. McGrail (editor), *Woodworking Techniques before AD 1500,* British Archaeological Reports, International Series 129, 1982, 169-85.

Army
Connolly, P. *Greece and Rome at War.* 1981.
Davies, R. W. *Service in the Roman Army.* Edited by D. J. Breeze and V. A. Maxfield. 1989.
Holder, P. A *The Roman Army in Britain.* 1982.
Jones, A. H. M. *The Later Roman Empire.* 1964. (Chapter 17.)
Luttwack, E. N. *The Grand Strategy of the Roman Empire from the First Century AD to the Third.* 1976; paperback 1979. See review by J. C. Mann, 'Power, Force and the Frontiers of the Empire', *Journal of Roman Studies* 69 (1979) 175-83.
Watson, G. R. *The Roman Soldier.* 1969.
Webster, G. *The Roman Imperial Army of the First and Second Centuries*

AD. Third edition, 1985.

Some individual sites

Bidwell, P. T. *The Legionary Bath-house and Basilica and Forum at Exeter*. 1979.

Bidwell, P. T. *The Roman Fort of Vindolanda*. 1985.

Birley, R. E. *Vindolanda, A Roman Frontier Post on Hadrian's Wall*. 1977.

Bishop, M. C., and Dore, J. N. *Corbridge, Excavations of the Roman Fort and Town, 1947-80*. Historic Buildings and Monuments Commission for England, Archaeological Report 8, 1988.

Curle, J. *A Roman Frontier Post and Its People, The Fort of Newstead*. 1911.

Dore, J, and Gillam, J. P. *The Roman Fort at South Shields, Excavations 1875-1975*. 1981.

Frere, S. S., and Wilkes, J. J. *Strageath, Excavations within the Roman Fort, 1973-86*. Britannia Monograph Series 9, 1989.

Hanson, W. S., and Yeoman, P. A. *Elginhaugh, A Roman Fort and Its Environs*. Edinburgh, 1987.

Philip, B. *The Excavation of the Roman Forts of the Classis Britannica at Dover 1970-1977*. 1981.

Manning, W. H. *Report on the Excavations at Usk 1965-76: The Fortress Excavations 1968-71*. 1981.

Pitts, L., and St Joseph, J. K. *Inchtuthil, The Legionary Fortress*. 1985.

Richmond, I. A. *Hod Hill: Volume 2, Excavations Carried Out Between 1951 and 1958*. 1968.

Robertson, A. S., Scott, M., and Keppie, L. *Bar Hill: A Roman Fort and Its Finds*. British Archaeological Reports 16, 1975.

Royal Commission on the Historical Monuments of England. *An Inventory of the Historical Monuments in the City of York: Volume 1, Eburacum, Roman York*. 1962.

Index

Aedes 26, 27, 28, 53. See also *Temples*
Altars 27, 40, 61
Ambleside, fort 59, 64
Amphitheatres 42, 43, 54, 65, 66
Annexes 38-40, 63
Antonine Wall 18, 19, 23, 24, 27, 38, 46, 47, 49, 61, 63
Aqueducts 36, 64
Ardoch, fort 5, 46, 60, 63
Artillery 59
Auxiliary units 7, 14, 15, 17, 23, 43
Barburgh Mill, fortlet 44, 46
Bar Hill, fort 61, 63, 70
Barrack-blocks 6, 8, 12, 17, 19, 20, 24, 33, 34, 35, 41, 42, 44, 46, 54, 60, 62, 64, 66. See also *Chalets*
Bastions 27, 66, 67
Bath-houses 8, 31, 36-8, 39, 42, 56, 63, 64, 65, 66
Bearsden, fort 24, 33, 37, 38, 39, 49, 63
Benwell, fort 20
Birrens, fort 25, 63
Burnswark, training area 52, 54, 63
Caerleon, legionary fortress 42, 43, 66
Caernarfon, fort 62, 65-6
Caesar 13, 16, 57
Camps 8, 9-11, 13, 22, 42, 47, 48, 53, 54, 58-9, 63, 65, 66, 68
Cardiff, fort 26, 66
Carpow, legionary base 19-20
Carrawburgh, fort and civil settlement 52, 65
Chalets 25, 33, 34, 64. See also *Barrack-blocks*
Chester, legionary fortress 58, 65
Chesterholm-*Vindolanda,* fort and civil settlement 28, 29, 30, 53, 56, 64, 70
Chesters, fort 28, 35, 38, 64
Chew Green, camp 11
Civil settlements 25, 55, 56-7, 64
Commanding officer's houses 8, 20, 25, 30, 31, 42, 62, 64, 65
Corbridge, legionary base 58, 64
Dalginross, camp 11
Defences. See under *Ditches, Ramparts* and *Walls*
De Metatione Castrorum 9

Ditches 7, 12, 16, 20, 25-7, 44, 45, 46, 47, 50, 59, 60, 61, 63, 66
Dover, fort 20, 70
Entrances, camp 10, 11
Food 31-2, 54, 59
Fortlets 43-4, 46, 63-4, 66, 69
Fortresses, legionary 13, 17, 19, 24, 41, 42, 63, 65, 66, 69, 70
Frontier control 13, 17, 18, 19
Gates 16, 20, 24, 25, 53, 56, 65, 67, 69
Granaries 8, 12, 20, 24, 25, 31-2, 41-2, 53, 54, 63, 64, 65, 69
Greatchesters, fort 36
Hadrian's Wall 5, 7, 18, 20, 24, 36, 37, 38, 46, 47, 56, 64, 68, 70
Hardknott, fort 40, 64
Headquarters buildings 6, 8, 17, 20, 25, 26, 27-31, 41, 42, 53, 62, 63, 64, 65
Hearths 54. See also *Ovens*
High Rochester, fort 59, 65
Hod Hill, fort 12, 66, 70
Hospitals 6, 8, 20, 25, 32, 41, 42
Housesteads, fort 5, 6-8, 25, 26, 29, 30, 32, 33, 36, 64
Inchtuthil, legionary fortress 41, 42, 46, 47, 48, 61, 63
Inscriptions 49, 50, 61
Josephus 51, 54
Kirkbuddo, camp 11, 63
Latrines 6, 8, 36, 37, 53, 54, 64, 66
Legions 13, 14, 17, 18, 41, 42, 47, 49, 58
Lunt, Baginton, fort 16, 31, 65 and cover
Lympne, fort 21, 66
Martinhoe, fortlet 43, 66
Materials of construction 13, 16, 18, 20, 21, 39, 42, 45, 46, 47-50, 60, 69
Metchley, fort 16
Nanstallon, fort 17
Newstead, fort 51, 52, 70
Numantia, siege works 13
Officers 14, 15, 27, 30, 31, 34, 40, 41, 42, 47, 53-4, 57, 58, 59
Old Carlisle, fort and civil settlement 55, 65
Ovens 24, 54
Parade ground 40, 54, 64

Parkneuk, watch-tower 45, 64
Pen Llystyn, fort 33
Pennymuir, camp 8, 63
Pevensey, fort 22, 61, 66-7
Planning, fort 7-8, 23-4
Portchester, fort 5, 21, 61, 67
Ramparts, turf or earth 7, 14, 16, 18, 19-20, 23, 24-5, 39, 44, 45, 46, 48, 50, 61, 63, 65
Reycross, camp 11, 65
Roads: camp 9
    forts 6-8, 12, 24, 31, 34, 41
Rough Castle, fort 27, 39, 63
Saxon Shore 5, 7, 21, 22, 26, 61, 66-7, 68
Scarborough, watch-tower 45, 65
Shrine. See *Aedes*
Signal-stations 46, 65
Siting, fort 47
Size, fort 17, 23, 47
South Shields, fort 12, 30, 64, 67, 70
Stables 8, 20, 24, 34, 54

Storehouses 8, 17, 19, 20, 24, 30, 34-6, 38, 41, 62. See also *Granaries*
Strongroom 8, 27, 28, 64. See also *Aedes* and *Headquarters building*
Supply bases 12, 64
Temples 26, 27, 28, 52, 53, 56, 65
Tents 9, 10, 16, 33, 34, 42, 48
Tools 47, 50-2
Towers, fort 16, 24-5. See also *Watch-towers*
Training area 52, 54, 63
Trajan's Column 47, 48, 49, 50, 59
Vegetius 49, 54
Walls, fort 7, 18, 20, 21, 23-4, 26, 42, 45, 46, 59, 62, 64-7
Watch-towers 45-6, 64, 65
Weapons 14, 30, 34, 50, 59
Winter quarters 15-17, 18
Workshops 6, 8, 17, 20, 24, 32, 41, 42, 62, 63, 64, 65
York, legionary fortress 24, 61, 65, 70